187239

PowerKids Readers:

The Bilingual Library of the United States of America

Bilingual Edition
English/Spanish
Edición bilingüe

NEW YORK
NUEVA YORK

JOSÉ MARÍA OBREGÓN

Traducción al español: María Cristina Brusca

The Rosen Publishing Group's
PowerKids Press™ & Editorial Buenas Letras™
New York

Published in 2005 by The Rosen Publishing Group, Inc.
29 East 21st Street, New York, NY 10010

First Edition

Photo Credits: Cover, pp. 21, 30 (Empire State Building) © Alan Schein Photography /Corbis; p. 5 © Joseph Sohm; ChromoSohm Inc./Corbis; p. 9 © National Geographic/Getty Images; pp. 11, 15, 17, 31 (Walt Whitman, Theodore Roosevelt, Julia Ward Howe, General Arnold, Slavery) © Bettmann/Corbis; p. 13 © PoodlesRock/Corbis; p. 19 © Gail Mooney/Corbis; p. 23 © Bob Krist/Corbis; pp. 25, 30 (New York State Capitol) © Lee Snider/Photo Images/Corbis; p. 26 © Bill Ross/Corbis; p. 30 (Bluebird) © Gary W. Carter/Corbis, p. 30 (Tree) © Robert Estall/Corbis, p. 30 (rock) © Dorling Kindersley/Getty Images; p. 31 (Franklin D. Roosevelt) © Corbis, p. 31 (Michael Jordan) © Duomo/Corbis, p. 31 (Oscar Hijuelos) ©Stephen J. Boitano/AP Wide World, p. 31 (harbor) © Charles E. Rotkin/Corbis.

Library of Congress Cataloging-in-Publication Data

Obregón, José María, 1963–
New York = Nueva York / José María Obregón.—1st ed.
   p. cm. — (The bilingual library of the United States of America)
Includes index.
ISBN 1-4042-3097-1 (library binding)
1. New York (State)—Juvenile literature. I. Title: Nueva York. II. Title. III. Series.
F119.3.O27 2006
974.7–dc22
                                     2004027123

Manufactured in the United States of America

Due to the changing nature of Internet links, Editorial Buenas Letras has developed an online list of Web sites related to the subject of this book. This site is updated regularly. Please use this link to access the list:

http://www.buenasletraslinks.com/ls/newyork

Contents

Contenido

Welcome to New York

New York is known as the Empire State. The flag and the seal of the state of New York have two female figures. They stand for freedom and justice.

Bienvenidos a Nueva York

Nueva York es conocido como el Estado Imperial. En la bandera y el escudo de Nueva York hay dos figuras femeninas. Estas figuras representan la libertad y la justicia.

New York State Flag and State Seal

Bandera y escudo de Nueva York

New York Geography

New York borders the states of Pennsylvania, New Jersey, Connecticut, Massachusetts, and Vermont. New York State also shares a border with Canada.

Geografía de Nueva York

Nueva York está limitado por los estados de Pennsylvania, Nueva Jersey, Connecticut, Massachusetts y Vermont. El Estado de Nueva York también comparte una frontera con Canadá.

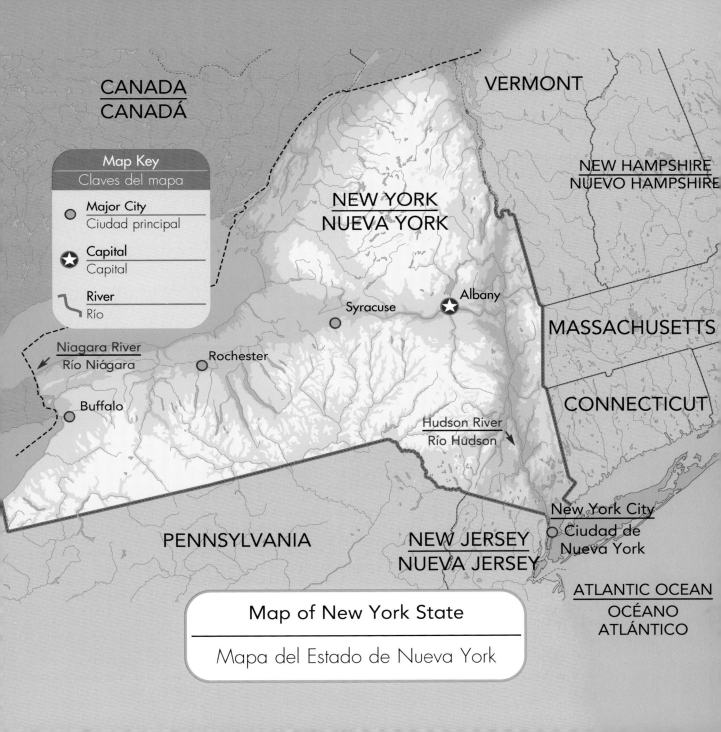

CANADA
CANADÁ

VERMONT

NEW HAMPSHIRE
NUEVO HAMPSHIRE

Map Key
Claves del mapa

Major City
Ciudad principal

Capital
Capital

River
Río

NEW YORK
NUEVA YORK

Albany

Syracuse

MASSACHUSETTS

Niagara River
Río Niágara

Rochester

CONNECTICUT

Buffalo

Hudson River
Río Hudson

New York City
Ciudad de
Nueva York

PENNSYLVANIA

NEW JERSEY
NUEVA JERSEY

ATLANTIC OCEAN
OCÉANO
ATLÁNTICO

Map of New York State

Mapa del Estado de Nueva York

New York State has many mountains, rivers, and forests. The Niagara River in the north forms the Niagara Falls. The Niagara Falls are on the border between the United States and Canada.

En el Estado de Nueva York hay muchos bosques, ríos y montañas. En el norte, el río Niágara forma las cataratas del Niágara. Las cataratas del Niágara están en la frontera entre los Estados Unidos y Canadá.

View of Niagara Falls

Vista de las cataratas del Niágara

New York History

Native American groups were the first to live in New York. In 1624, the Dutch came to live in New York. The Native Americans and the Dutch traded furs and other goods.

Historia de Nueva York

Los primeros habitantes de Nueva York fueron los nativos americanos. En 1624, los holandeses vinieron a vivir a Nueva York. Los nativos cambiaban pieles por las mercancías que traían los holandeses.

Landing of Dutch Colony on Staten Island

Colonia holandesa en Staten Island

In 1664, the British took control of the region. New Yorkers fought for their independence. In 1777, New Yorkers won an important battle, the Battle of Saratoga.

En 1664, los ingleses tomaron posesión de la región. Los neoyorquinos lucharon por su independencia. En 1777, los neoyorquinos ganaron una batalla muy importante: la Batalla de Saratoga.

Surrender of Burgoyne, Saratoga, October 17, 1777

El General Burgoyne se rinde en Saratoga

George Washington was named the first president of the United States in New York City. The act took place in Federal Hall on April 30, 1789.

George Washington fue nombrado primer presidente de los Estados Unidos en la Ciudad de Nueva York. La ceremonia tuvo lugar en el Federal Hall, el 30 de abril de 1789.

George Washington Becomes President of the United States

George Washington se convierte en presidente de los Estados Unidos

Sojourner Truth was born into slavery in New York in 1797. She escaped slavery in 1826. Sojourner worked all her adult life against slavery and for women's rights.

Sojourner Truth nació esclava, en Nueva York, en 1797. En 1826, escapó de la esclavitud. Durante toda su vida adulta, Sojourner luchó en contra de la esclavitud y por los derechos de las mujeres.

Sojourner Truth

The Statue of Liberty stands on Liberty Island in New York Harbor. The statue was a gift from France to America. The Statue of Liberty represents peace and freedom.

La Estatua de la Libertad se encuentra en la isla Liberty, en el puerto de Nueva York. La estatua fue un regalo de Francia a los Estados Unidos. La Estatua de la Libertad simboliza la paz y la libertad.

The Statue of Liberty
_____
La Estatua de la Libertad

Living in New York

New York City is the most-populated city in the United States. More than 8 million people live in the city. People live and work in very tall buildings.

La vida en Nueva York

La Ciudad de Nueva York es la más populosa de los Estados Unidos. Más de 8 millones de personas viven en esta ciudad. La gente vive y trabaja en edificios muy altos.

Manhattan's Skyscrapers

Rascacielos en Manhattan

Manhattan is one of New York City's five boroughs. Manhattan is known as the Big Apple. Manhattan has many museums, theaters, and parks.

Manhattan es uno de los cinco distritos de la Ciudad de Nueva York. Manhattan es conocida como la Gran Manzana. Manhattan tiene muchos parques, museos y teatros.

ANCIENT ART
FROM THE
SHUMEI FAMILY
COLLECTION

Winslow
Homer

THE
GUBBIO
STUDIOLO

Early
Greek
Art

Toulouse-Lautrec

The Metropolitan Museum of Art in Manhattan

El Museo Metropolitano de Arte en Manhattan

New York City, Buffalo, and Syracuse are important cities in New York. Albany is the capital of New York State.

Nueva York, Buffalo y Syracuse son ciudades importantes del Estado de Nueva York. La capital del Estado de Nueva York es Albany.

The Capitol Building in Albany

Capitolio en la ciudad de Albany

Activity:
Let's Draw the State Flower
The rose is the New York State flower.

Actividad:
Dibujemos la flor del estado
La rosa es la flor del Estado de Nueva York.

1

Draw a circle for the center of the rose. Add curved shapes around the center as shown

Dibuja un círculo para hacer el centro de la rosa. Añade algunas formas curvas alrededor del centro, como en el modelo.

2

Add twelve more petal shapes as shown.

Agrega doce pétalos más, siguiendo el ejemplo.

3

Now add another layer
of petals.

Ahora añade otra capa
de pétalos.

4

Erase extra lines. Add a
stem and leaves.

Borra las líneas que sobran.
Agrega un tallo y unas hojas.

5

Add shading and detail
to your rose.

Sombrea y agrega detalles
a tu rosa.

Timeline

Cronología

Native Americans arrive in what is now New York.	**12,000 BC/AC**	Los nativos americanos llegan a lo que hoy es el Estado de Nueva York.
Giovanni da Verrazano becomes the first European explorer to reach New York.	**1524**	Giovanni de Verrazano es el primer europeo en explorar Nueva York.
Dutch settlers establish a colony at Fort Orange (now Albany).	**1624**	Los holandeses establecen una colonia en Fort Orange (hoy, Albany).
The British take New York from the Dutch.	**1663**	Los ingleses vencen a los holandeses y toman el Estado de Nueva York.
New York becomes the eleventh state in the Union.	**1788**	Nueva York se convierte en el undécimo estado de la Unión.
The Brooklyn Bridge opens.	**1883**	Se inaugura el puente de Brooklyn.
The World Trade Center is destroyed in a terrorist attack.	**2001**	El World Trade Center es destruído por un ataque terrorista.

New York Events	Eventos en Nueva York
January to March Sky-jumping competition in Lake Placid	Enero a marzo Competencia de salto de esquí, en Lake Placid
February Westminster Kennel Club Dog Show in New York City	Febrero Exhibición canina del Westminster Kennel Club, en la Ciudad de Nueva York
March St. Patrick's Day Parade in New York City	Marzo Desfile del Día de San Patricio, en la Ciudad de Nueva York
May Festival of Lilacs in Rochester	Mayo Festival de las lilas, en Rochester
June Belmont Stakes Horse Race on Long Island	Junio Carrera de caballos Belmont Stakes, en Long Island
September Adirondack Hot Air Balloon Festival in Glens Falls	Septiembre Festival Adirondack de globos, en Glens Falls
November Thanksgiving Day Parade in New York City	Noviembre Desfile del Día de Acción de Gracias, en la Ciudad de Nueva York
December Rockefeller Center Tree Lighting Ceremony in New York City	Diciembre Ceremonia de iluminación del árbol de Navidad, en el Rockefeller Center, en la Ciudad de Nueva York

New York Facts/Datos sobre Nueva York

Population
19 million

Población
19 millones

Capital
Albany

Capital
Albany

State Motto
Excelsior (Ever upward)

Lema del estado
Excelsior (siempre hacia arriba)

State Flower
Rose

Flor del estado
Rosa

State Bird
Bluebird

Ave del estado
Azulejo

State Nickname
The Empire State

Mote del estado
El Estado Imperial

State Tree
Sugar Maple

Árbol del estado
Arce

State Song
"I Love New York"

Canción del estado
"Amo Nueva York"

State Gemstone
Garnet

Piedra preciosa
Granate

Famous New Yorkers/Neoyorquinos famosos

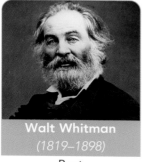

Walt Whitman
(1819–1898)

Poet
Poeta

Theodore Roosevelt
(1858–1919)

U.S. President
Presidente de E. U. A.

Julia Ward Howe
(1819–1910)

Social Reformer
Reformista social

Franklin D. Roosevelt
(1882–1945)

U.S. President
Presidente de E. U. A.

Oscar Hijuelos
(1951–   )

Author
Escritor

Michael Jordan
(1963–   )

Basketball Player
Jugador de baloncesto

Words to Know/Palabras que debes saber

<u>battle</u>
batalla

<u>border</u>
frontera

<u>harbor</u>
puerto

<u>slavery</u>
esclavitud

Here are more books to read about New York:
Otros libros que puedes leer sobre Nueva York:

In English/En inglés:
New York
By Cotter, Kristin
Children's Press, 2002

In Spanish/En español:
Nueva York, el estado imperial
Ball, Jackie y Behrens, Kristen
Traducción Victory Productions
World Almanac Library, 2004

Words in English: 296

Palabras en español: 336

Index

Índice